CONTENTS

THE MIDDLE AGES

The medieval period, or middle ages, is the name historians give to the period of time that links the ancient world, which ended with the fall of the Roman Empire in the 5th century, to the modern world, which began with the Renaissance in the 15th century.

THE DARK AGES

For several centuries the Romans controlled much of Europe, keeping order and bringing some unity to its various peoples. When their empire fell, many of their technological skills and advances were lost as Europe was divided between competing warlords. Almost a thousand years later the Renaissance heralded a new interest in science and learning.

The early medieval period – from around 500–1000 AD is sometimes referred to as the Dark Ages. This reflected the idea that the people of the time had fallen into a life of hardship and ignorance. Today's historians still refer to the period as the Dark Ages, but only in the sense that much of what happened then is unknown to us.

During this unsettled period, techniques such as metalworking and pottery making declined for a while and so people left little evidence of their way of life for archaeologists to find. People during this time made their homes and their belongings largely from wood, which has since rotted away.

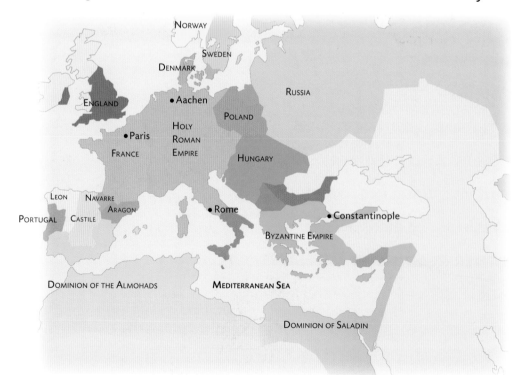

This map shows countries and empires in the medieval world around 1190 AD. The Holy Roman Empire was Christian, while the Dominions of Saladin and the Almohads were ruled by Muslims. England, France, Norway and Portugal were kingdoms.

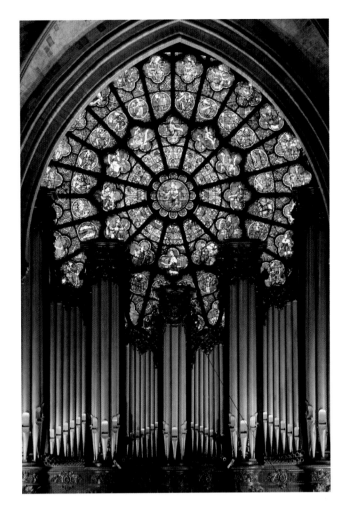

One of the rose windows in Chartres Cathedral, France.

Gradually, the peoples of Europe flourished and communities grew, increasing their trade with each other. New rulers such as Charles the Great, or Charlemagne (742–814), began to reunite people and to revive and rediscover knowledge from Roman and Greek times. The idea that people belonged to nations rather than tribes began to grow.

CRISIS AND COMMERCE

The Middle Ages came to a close in crisis as the Black Death swept into Europe in the mid-14th century. In some places this epidemic killed as many as two-thirds of the people, who were already weakened by food shortages.

The survivors rebuilt their communities and prospered. Workers demanded more pay and more freedoms. The cities of medieval Europe grew into strong financial and commercial centres, trading across the world.

VOYAGES OF DISCOVERY

Towards the end of the 15th century ocean-going ships were equipped with compasses, effective rudders and sails that worked in every kind of wind. Their voyages of discovery were a turning point in history, and carried Europe out of the Middle Ages and into the modern world.

The Bayeux Tapestry shows William the Conqueror killing King Harold of England at the Battle of Hastings in 1066.

BUILDING HOMES

The great majority of people in medieval times lived in very simple homes. Most often, these were dwellings with one or two rooms that were shared by several members of a family – and sometimes their animals, too. Many wealthy people lived in castles or in large houses in the towns or in manor houses in the country.

BUILDING MATERIALS

The most common building materials for medieval homes were wattle and daub. A frame was built by first driving wooden posts into the ground. Secondary timbers, called withies, were nailed or tied across the uprights to give additional strength. Next, a number of thinner branches, called wattles, were woven in and out of the posts to form the walls of the house. Two people working together pressed in the daub – a mixture of mud, straw and often horse and cow dung – from both sides of the wall at the same time. Once the daub had dried it was plastered with a mixture of sand and lime.

STOPPING THE ROT

Wattle-and-daub homes didn't last long because the posts rotted away. In the 13th century a line of stones, called the plinth, was added to keep the wood away from the damp ground and so houses stood for longer. The stone line of the plinth was laid along the line of the walls, and partly buried in the ground, and a heavy rectangular wooden sill added on top. Upright posts for the house were fixed to the sill using joints and wooden pegs.

English dwellings built in the style of 13th-century medieval cottages can be seen at the Weald and Downland Museum, Sussex.

A thatcher repairs the straw on the roof of a thatched house in Milton Abbas, England.

assembled on the ground, then hoisted into a vertical position. This was difficult, but it meant that the walls of the house could be built with lighter timbers, as they didn't need to support the roof.

TIMBER FRAMING

In a timber-framed house the timbers are joined to form a support for the roof. The most common type of construction was the box frame. This used both horizontal and vertical timbers to assemble a box-like structure that supported the roof and walls of the building.

The cruck frame used a pair of curved timbers (the crucks) to support the weight of the roof. The box frame was assembled in position, one timber at a time, but cruck frames were

A cruck frame in a medieval house.

Cathedral building

After the fall of the Roman Empire many construction skills were lost and no large buildings were created. This changed when order started to return at the end of the 8th century and strong rulers directed the building of magnificent cathedrals – Charlemagne's cathedral at Aachen in Germany is the oldest in northern Europe.

Building in stone

The stones for building cathedrals came from quarries, either by barge along rivers or hauled along the roads on carts pulled by teams of oxen. Deep foundations had to be laid in the ground to support the massive weight of the cathedral and the walls were thick and strong.

The builders constructed scaffolding around the building as it grew in height. Stones were carved and shaped on the ground before being hauled up the scaffolding using a windlass or a pulley. A windlass is like a horizontal cylinder that can be turned with a crank. As it turns it winds up the rope that carries the stones.

The treadwheel crane

Towards the end of the medieval period the treadwheel crane was reintroduced. Men operated a treadmill to provide the lifting power for these cranes, which had not been

The magnificent Rouen Cathedral, France, shows the great skills of medieval architects and stonemasons.

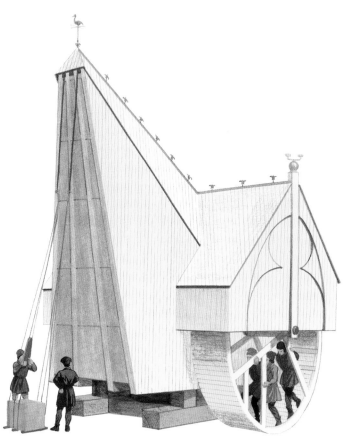

used since the fall of the Roman Empire. They had a major part in building cathedrals. However, medieval cranes could only lift weights vertically, unlike modern cranes which can also swing the load horizontally.

GOTHIC CATHEDRALS

The greatest medieval cathedrals were built in the Gothic style, starting in the middle of the 12th century. The builders erected high arches and soaring towers, with flying

buttresses on the outside of the cathedral to support the weight of the roof. Flying buttresses started from the top of the wall and carried the weight of the roof away from the building to the ground. They allowed the walls to be lighter, with larger windows, because they no longer supported the roof.

The Palatine Chapel in Aachen Cathedral is where Charlemagne is buried and where many kings and queens were crowned.

STAINED GLASS

The huge windows in many Gothic cathedrals were ornamented with beautiful stained glass. They are like mosaics of coloured glass joined with lead to illustrate Bible stories for the many members of the congregation who could not read. The windows were assembled on a wooden board and enclosed within a frame before being lifted into position.

11

MASTER MASONS

Medieval masons were highly skilled craftsmen and respected members of society. Every mason was an architect, builder, designer and engineer. Using simple tools, a knowledge of geometry and experience of materials, master masons created some remarkable and awe-inspiring buildings.

MIXING AND MORTARING

The mortar that fixed the stones together was prepared by burning limestone or chalk in kilns to produce quicklime. This was mixed with water, making a lime putty, and sand was added. The mixture was then put into a mixer. This was a circular well with a vertical centre post attached to a horizontal beam with paddles. The vertical post was rotated to turn the horizontal beam so the paddles stirred the mixture into mortar.

Lime mortar took a long time to set, so building work was slow. The builders had to wait for one layer to set before adding another, or the weight of the new stones would have pushed out the mortar in the layer below. According to some estimates,

A modern stonemason cleans a sculpture on the outside of Notre Dame Cathedral in Paris, France.

Master masons created the beautiful vaulted ceiling inside the Cathedral of St Pierre in Beauvais, France.

medieval buildings grew on average between about 20 to 50 centimetres a day.

Seasonal work

Skilled tradesmen and apprentices learning their craft did much of the building work under the close supervision of the master mason. Most of this work was carried out during spring and summer. In winter the masons carved a fresh supply of stone for the building work that restarted the following spring, while the mortar was left to set properly on the work already completed.

Stonecutting

Using compasses and a set square, the master mason drew all the patterns he needed to cut the full size stones and used them to create wooden templates. The stonecutter then took a suitable block of stone, squared it to size and drew the outline of the template

on each end of the block. He then cut it to the required shape. Stonemasons today still use templates, but they are more likely to be made of plastic than of wood.

A medieval stonemason used tools that are familiar to masons today, who still use compasses for their designs and metal chisels and hammers to carve the blocks of stone.

Mason's symbol

Each master stonemason had a special symbol. When he worked on a building, his symbol was cut into every block of stone he carved. This was a record of all the work he had done on the project and he was paid accordingly.

13

FARMING

The lives of most medieval Europeans revolved around the seasons and the farming year. Farmers rotated their crops and the hard work of tilling the soil was made easier by devices such as heavy ploughs, horse collars and whippletrees.

A farmer uses a wheeled plough in this 15th-century illustration from The Book of Hours *by Duc de Berry.*

THE THREE-FIELD SYSTEM

Medieval farmers practised a system of crop rotation. They set aside one field for sheep and cattle to graze. They grew one crop, such as wheat, in a second field and another crop, such as beans, in a third field. The following year the field that had been grazed was planted with wheat, the wheat field was planted with beans, while the bean field had no crop but was grazed. In this way, each field recovered its fertility and was naturally fertilized by the grazing animals.

THE HEAVY PLOUGH

The clay soils of Northern Europe were too heavy for light ploughs that only scratched the surface. The heavy, wheeled plough that was developed during medieval times made all the difference. It had a heavy blade, called a coulter, to dig deep into the ground. Some of these ploughs were so heavy they were pulled by a team of oxen or horses. Peasant farmers who could not afford a team of oxen joined their neighbours, each contributing an ox to make up the team.

14

Every year, most farmers had to give much of their produce to the landowner in payment for using the land.

HARNESSING HORSES

Ancient methods of harnessing a horse didn't allow it to use its full strength because the strap placed around its neck made it choke when it pulled hard. The breast strap introduced in Germany in the 6th century allowed the horse to use much more power but the strap still moved up to its neck.

The horse collar that came into use in Europe during the 9th century was strapped around the shoulders and chest so the horse could pull with all its strength without choking.

Farmers continued to use oxen because horses were more expensive and needed more care. But horses were faster than oxen and could be worked for longer so the collar meant that more horses were used by farmers.

THE ACRE

Fields were divided into strips of land that a farmer could plough in one day. This area became the acre, a unit of measurement equivalent to 4,046 square metres. Each strip was a furlong (a long furrow) in length, which was a little more than 200 metres. This was roughly the distance that could be ploughed before the team had to stop and rest.

THE WHIPPLETREE

The whippletree (or whiffletree) first appeared Europe during the 11th century. It had one or more crossbars that linked a cart, wagon or plough to the draught animals in front. A whippletree allowed a ploughman to harness together more than one horse or ox and to turn more easily at the edge of a field.

A whippletree has one or more crossbars attached to the harnesses of the oxen or horses in front.

FOOD ON THE TABLE

A medieval baker takes loaves from his oven in this 15th-century illustration.

People in medieval times enjoyed a varied diet. Peasants ate bread, porridge, stews, vegetables and some meat. They grew beans, barley, rye and wheat, as well as onions, radishes, carrots, parsnips and turnips in the family garden. They also collected nuts and berries, and caught fish whenever they could.

AN OPEN FIRE

Most cooking was done over an open fire in a fireplace that was usually a circle of stones in the middle of a one-room home. The fire gave warmth, light and heat for cooking.

Boiling and stewing were done in one pot so they were the most economical ways of preparing food. A cast-iron cauldron was placed in the middle of the fire, either sitting on legs or hung from a hook attached to a roof beam. Earthenware cookpots were put in the ashes beside the fire or placed on a flat stone over the fire.

DAILY BREAD

Most people in medieval Europe ate between 1 and 1.5 kilograms of bread a day. It was not easy for them to make bread at home so the baker became an important member of every community. Often, people prepared bread dough at home and then brought it to be baked in the baker's oven.

The oven was a large rounded chamber, a few metres across and built from brick or clay. It was filled with wood, which was lit and allowed to burn until the oven reached the required temperature. At that point the ashes were raked out, the bread was placed inside on the baking shelves and the oven sealed up to preserve the heat.

Food preservation

Food preservation works by stopping, or at least slowing down, the action of the microorganisms that cause food to decay. One way to do this is by freezing, but that wasn't an option in medieval times as there was no refrigeration.

Another method was to dry food. In warmer areas around the Mediterranean fruit was dried in the sun before being stored in cellars and then eaten in the winter. Further north the drying was done in ovens.

Smoking and salting

To avoid the expense of feeding livestock in the winter people slaughtered animals in the autumn and preserved the meat. They smoked meat by hanging it in a chimney. This killed bacteria, dried the meat and flavoured it, too. Salting food was also common. Meat, fish and vegetables were layered in salt and stored in earthenware pots for winter use. Pickling or brining food preserved it in a salty liquid, to which vinegar was sometimes added.

A fish merchant inspects fillets of cod, whiting and haddock in a present-day smokehouse.

Wind and Watermills

For thousands of years people ground their grain into flour with a handmill, which consisted of a flat stone to hold the seed and a grinding stone that rolled and crushed them. The process became much easier when people discovered how to harness wind and water to turn the grinding stone.

Windmills

Grinding grain to make flour for bread was one of the few tasks that were mechanized in the medieval period. Windmills made this possible. They were invented in the Middle East in the 7th century AD and introduced in Europe during the 12th century. A typical European windmill had a system of gears that transmitted the energy of the upright sails as they turned in the wind to a vertical shaft. This shaft turned the heavy millstones that ground the grain.

At first, the whole mill was turned to face the wind by a long pole attached to a vertical post in the middle of the mill. These post mills were replaced in the 14th century by windmills with sails mounted on a rotating cap – only the cap was turned to the wind.

Watermills

By the 1st century AD water-powered mills were common throughout the Mediterranean region. Two types of vertical wheel were used. An undershot

The sails on this English windmill are mounted on a rotating cap.

wheel sat in a stream and was pushed around by the force of the water rushing by. When the water level was low, an undershot wheel did not work well. An overshot wheel had a pipe or channel that directed a stream of water on to the top of the wheel.

Like the turning sails of the windmill, the waterwheel turned a driveshaft, which turned the millstones. By the 10th century watermills were powering the heavy industry of Europe. They were not only used to grind grain, but also to power bellows for furnaces and trip hammers for working metal.

TIDE MILLS

A tide mill is a type of watermill that is driven by the rise and fall of the tides. People constructed a dam across a river estuary or a

The undershot watermill at Braine le Château, Belgium, was built in the 12th century.

tidal inlet to create a reservoir of water. They then controlled the flow of water into and out of the reservoir with a sluice gate which they opened and closed.

As the tide came in, the gate was opened so the water filled a millpond. When the tide began to go out the gate was closed, storing water in the pond. Once the tide was low enough the gate was opened so the stored water flowed out and turned the waterwheel.

The Nendrum Monastery mill was built on an island in Strangford Lough in Northern Ireland. It dates from 787 AD and is one of the earliest tide mills.

19

THE AGE OF WOOD

Wood was an essential material in the Middle Ages. A great many everyday items – from house frames to furniture and food bowls – were made of wood. In fact, wood was so important that the medieval period has been described as the age of wood.

Medieval houses with timber frames line a street in Rouen, France.

CUTTING TIMBER

Two main tools were used for cutting timber – an axe to fell trees and a smaller bill hook to trim off branches. Woodcutters stripped bark with a two-handed draw knife pulled along the wood. If the bark came from trees that contained tannin, such as oak and elm, it was used to make leather from animal hides.

Saws weren't very common, especially in the early medieval period, as they were too expensive and difficult to maintain for most village carpenters. An axe and an adze were used to trim and shape timber. This could be quite a wasteful process, although leftover bits of wood were used for making charcoal.

THE POLE LATHE

The lathe, a tool used for turning wood so it can be shaped, probably dates back to Egyptian times. Often, lathes were powered by an assistant pulling a cord back and forth, but in medieval Europe woodturners preferred to use the pole lathe. The frame of a pole lathe was usually big enough for the turner to stand as he worked on a piece of wood, which

The power to turn the pole lathe comes from the springy wooden pole that is linked to the foot treadle.

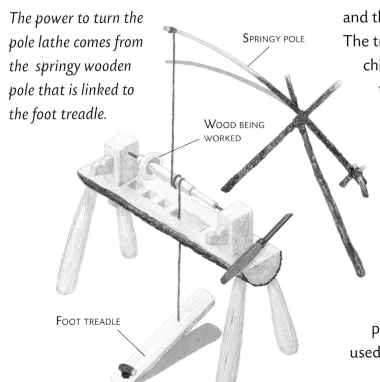

SPRINGY POLE

WOOD BEING WORKED

FOOT TREADLE

and the piece of wood was set spinning. The turner cut into the wood with his chisel on this down stroke. When he took his foot off the treadle, the pole straightened and pulled up the rope.

The spring pole lathe was easy to build and could be made both light and portable, or assembled quickly from local materials. However, the turning speeds were slow and the pole lathe could not turn very large pieces of wood. Pole lathes were popular for several centuries and are used by some traditional craftsmen today.

he secured on sharp metal spikes between two upright posts called poppets or puppets.

One end of a cord was attached overhead to a pole of springy wood. The other end was wrapped around the piece, then attached to a foot treadle. When the turner pressed his foot down on the treadle the pole bent a little

A furniture maker in Arkansas, USA, uses a pole lathe.

GREEN TIMBER

Carpenters often worked timber when it was 'green', which meant that it was not seasoned and had not dried out before it was used. One advantage of using green timber was that a carpenter could split it fairly easily with wedges.

TEXTILES

Wool was very valuable in medieval Europe and the finest wool came from England. A thriving industry exported wool from England to spinners and weavers in the rest of Europe. The Lord Chancellor in the House of Lords still sits on the Woolsack, a tradition dating back to the Middle Ages.

FROM FLEECE TO CLOTH

Before the woollen fleece of an animal could be turned into cloth it was first washed, then combed to smooth out and untangle the fibres. Next, the yarn was spun with a distaff and a drop spindle. A distaff was a stick with a fork or comb on the tip to hold the wool fibres while they were spun on to the drop spindle. A spindle was a weighted stick that was set spinning to wind the thread as it was fed from the distaff.

THE SPINNING WHEEL

No one knows for sure where the spinning wheel was invented – perhaps in China, India or the Middle East. When it appeared in medieval Europe in the 13th century some people looked on it with suspicion.

A spinning wheel produced thread more quickly than a drop spindle, but the thread was neither twisted enough nor even in appearance. The problem was that the spinner had to use one hand to spin the wheel (by pushing a stick against the spokes or by turning a crank) and only had one hand to feed in the fibres. About 300 years passed before the spinning wheel improved enough to take over from the distaff and spindle method in Europe.

A woman spins her wheel with one hand and feeds the fibres with the other in this illustration from a medieval manuscript.

People are shown collecting fruit and playing games on an embroidered French tapestry.

WHAT PEOPLE WORE

Most people wore clothes of rough wool or linen, and rarely had more than two outfits. Men wore tunics over long woollen leggings and women wore long woollen dresses and stockings. Clothes were usually brown, red or grey, and were seldom washed, although undergarments were regularly cleaned. Both men and women wore shoes of thick cloth or leather, or wooden clogs. Woollen hats, mittens and cloaks kept out the cold in winter.

FULLING

Newly-woven cloth was beaten in water to shrink and thicken it. This process was called fulling. It was laborious when done by hand, but in the 12th century fulling mills made the job much easier.

A fulling mill had a revolving drum turned by water power. The cloth was placed inside the drum where wooden hammers beat it more effectively than a man with a club could manage. After fulling, it was stretched out for drying, then brushed to a smooth finish.

A waterwheel in a fulling mill turns the drum and hammers beat the cloth.

IRONWORKING

Iron has been an essential metal for making things for more than 3,000 years. Although iron ore was plentiful and freely available, extracting iron from the ore was not easy. Every medieval village and castle had a blacksmith who made horseshoes, hand tools, iron ploughshares, door hinges and other useful items.

PROCESSING ORE

For much of the Middle Ages iron was obtained in the same way as it had been since ancient times. Iron melts at a higher temperature than the Romans achieved in their furnaces. The ironworkers of the Middle Ages found a way of obtaining iron from its ore without melting it. They washed the ore, and then roasted it, heating it to burn off impurities.

Next, they broke the ore into smaller pieces and put it with charcoal in a furnace called a bloomery. The burning charcoal produced a gas called carbon monoxide, which reacted with the iron

ore and removed oxygen from it. The end result was a spongy mass of red hot, but still solid, iron called a bloom. The major

A female blacksmith grips a piece of red-hot iron and beats it with a hammer.

24

problem with the bloomery process was that it produced only small amounts of iron – just a couple of kilograms – at a time.

Working iron

The bloom was hammered into wrought iron on an anvil. A piece of iron was strengthened with carbon by placing it in contact with charcoal as it was being worked. Carbon from the charcoal was absorbed by the iron during this process. When it was red hot wrought iron was easily shaped by hammering it.

Cast iron

Around the 11th century, some watermills that ground grain were used in ironmaking. The waterwheels were altered so they could operate trip hammers that broke up ore more efficiently than by hand.

Watermills were also used to power furnace bellows, allowing much higher temperatures to be reached than had been possible before.

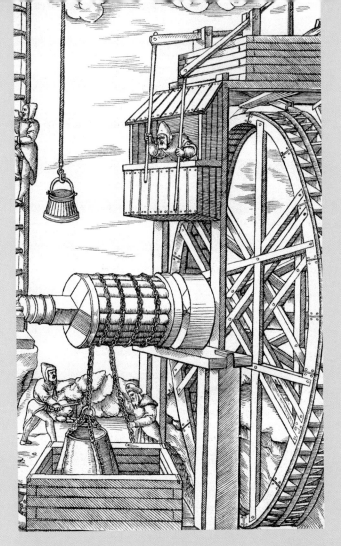

The power of a watermill was used to crush large quantities of rocks.

From the early 14th century people started to build larger furnaces that could reach the high temperatures required to convert iron ore into molten metal and produce cast iron.

People soon learned how to produce wrought iron or cast iron by adjusting the amount of air, and therefore oxygen, they let into their furnaces. Cast iron is hard and strong, but it is more brittle than wrought iron and wrought iron was still preferred for many uses.

Blast furnaces for making cast iron were expensive to build and maintain compared with bloomeries and so wrought-iron production continued at most ironworks.

Hoof protection

The hoofs of domesticated horses needed protection from wear and tear. Early horseshoes were tied to a horse's hoofs. By the Middle Ages the practice of nailing shoes to hoofs was common and, by the 13th century, the manufacture of iron horseshoes was widespread.

25

MANUSCRIPTS AND SCRIBES

For much of the medieval period, men called scribes wrote books by hand. A book written by hand is called a manuscript. (A book typed out on a keyboard is called a typescript.) Manuscripts were mostly written on parchment or vellum made from animal skins.

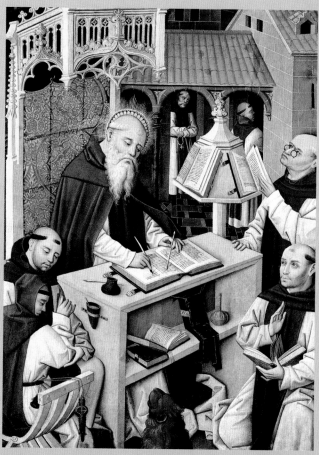

Scribes work in a scriptorium, *which is a place for writing, usually in a monastery.*

PARCHMENT AND VELLUM

Parchment and vellum are made from the skins of calves, goats or sheep. Vellum is a higher quality parchment. Parchment differed from leather in the way it was prepared. The first step was to soak the skins in water to clean them. Next, they were softened in a bath of lime for a week so the hair could be removed more easily. Lime burns unprotected skin, so the animal hides were stirred with long wooden poles.

The skins were rinsed and returned to the lime bath for a shorter soak, then carefully rinsed again. They were tied to a wooden frame and left to stretch. The stretched skins were scraped with curved knives to remove any hair and to reduce the parchment to the required thickness.

GETTING READY TO WRITE

A large sheet of parchment was cut into several smaller pages. Each page was rubbed smooth with a pumice stone to prepare it for writing. The writing materials were a quill pen, made from the feather of a bird, such as a goose, and red and black inks.

The scribe also kept a sharp knife to scrape any mistakes off the parchment, and another knife to keep his quill sharp. Before beginning to write the scribe ruled the parchment to ensure his work was neat and evenly spaced.

A modern parchment maker stretches a skin over a wooden frame.

THE BOOK OF KELLS

A remarkable illuminated manuscript is the *Book of Kells* in the library of Trinity College in Dublin. It was probably created by monks around 800 AD, then taken to the Abbey of Kells in Ireland. It was never completed.

ILLUMINATED MANUSCRIPTS

Sometimes, the text of a manuscript was given decorated borders, ornate initial letters and illustrations that were often picked out in gold and silver. These illustrated manuscripts were first made between the 4th and 5th centuries AD. Most illuminated manuscripts were created on vellum in a time-consuming and expensive process, so they were usually made for special books such as the Bible.

Most books in the early Middle Ages were produced in monasteries. An illustrator started when a scribe had completed his work. He worked out designs on wax tablets, then carefully transferred them to the vellum. The artists used several tools, including compasses, graphite for drawing the initial outline of the illustration, and various brushes for applying coloured inks or paints.

This illuminated manuscript depicts a medieval fair.

THE PRINTING PRESS

The invention of the printing press in Europe in the 15th century was a very important moment in history. It marked the time when the medieval period ended and the Renaissance began. Soon, books were printed quickly and in large numbers, and fewer and fewer were written laboriously by hand.

BLOCK BOOKS

From the end of the 6th century, Chinese printers cut blocks from wood and carved and inked their surfaces to print patterns on textiles and short religious texts on paper. Medieval craftsmen did the same and carved scenes and stories on to wooden blocks. These block books were much cheaper and faster to make than hand-copied versions, and they became very popular. One of the best known was called *The Bible of the Poor*. The blocks didn't last long so only a limited number of pages were printed from each.

LETTER SETS

Johannes Gutenberg, who came from Mainz, Germany, had the idea of creating reusable type. This involved making individual letter blocks that were set up to form a page of type for printing, then broken up and reused

A replica of the printing press used by Johannes Gutenberg.

A modern printing press in action at the Georgia Pacific paper mill in the USA.

to form another, completely different page. He began work on his printing press around 1436. His first letter sets were carved from wood. The problem with using wood was that the letters quickly became worn out and unusable. After some experimenting with metals, Gutenberg settled on an alloy of lead, tin and antimony as the best material for his type, and was soon casting the letters in moulds he designed himself.

GUTENBERG BIBLE

The Gutenberg Bible is also known as the 42-line Bible, because 42 lines of text were printed on each page. Gutenberg probably started work on the Bible around 1450 and finished copies were ready by 1455. Gutenberg is thought to have produced about 180 copies of the Bible, of which 48 are known to exist today.

INKS AND PAPER

The water-based inks used at the time weren't suitable for the printing press. Gutenberg developed an oil-based ink from lampblack and linseed oil that was much more durable. Finally, in 1455, he produced the first printed Bible. Gutenberg printed on vellum and on paper. Paper was just becoming available in large quantities in Europe, having been introduced earlier from China by way of the Middle East. Paper production in Italy and Germany dates from around 1400.

WOODEN PLATES

The printing press was modelled on the wine-and-olive presses of the Mediterranean. The type was mounted on a wooden plate, or platen, then inked and the paper laid on top. A long handle turned a heavy wooden screw, pressing the paper down against the type. Using this method a printer produced about 250 single-sided sheets in an hour. The wooden printing press remained largely unchanged for more than 300 years.

MOVING AROUND

Travelling from place to place in the Middle Ages was not easy. Many Roman roads, such as Watling Street, still survived, but they had fallen into disrepair as no one took responsibility for maintaining them. There were few advances in road transport technology during the medieval period.

RELYING ON HORSES

Horses were a vital part of medieval society – in agriculture and warfare, and as a means of transport. A good riding horse, able to carry a rider smoothly over the rough roads and paths between places, was of great value.

Packhorses were used to carry goods and belongings in panniers or sidebags. They were especially good where road surfaces were poor and wheeled vehicles couldn't be used. Carriages were rare. Horse-drawn carts hauled goods over short distances. Carthorses were powerful, stocky animals, able to pull loads of around 250 kilograms each.

ROAD REVIVAL

As Europe gradually recovered from the collapse of the Roman Empire, the growing cities began to trade with each other again. By the 15th century, well-maintained roads had become essential to bring a variety of goods into the cities to supply the needs of their growing populations.

One of the first major roads to be established in the medieval period was the Varangian Road. This was a trade route set up by the Vikings of Scandinavia in the 9th century and it linked the ports in the Baltic Sea to the Middle East by way of Russia.

A stone packhorse bridge crosses a stream at Watendlath in the Lake District.

CANAL BUILDING

Building canals came to a halt after the fall of Rome, but was revived as trading increased. Waterways linked rivers using flash locks in the weirs of watermills. Upright timbers supported a set of boards, called paddles, against the current. When the paddles were removed boats coming downstream were carried through on the sudden rush, or flash, of water. Boats travelling upstream were winched or towed through the lock.

The introduction of the pound lock around the 14th century did away with the need to use a winch. By opening and closing the gates of the pound lock to control the water level, a boat could be floated upstream.

A lock on the Ille et Rance canal in Brittany, France.

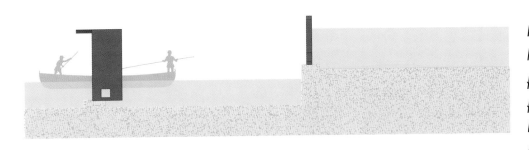

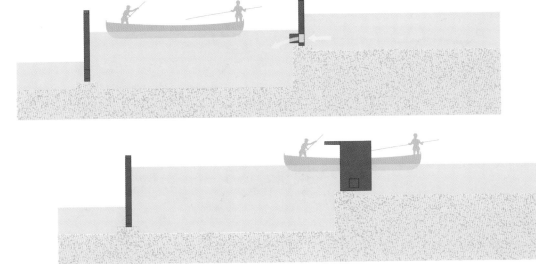

Paddles control the level of water in the pound section of a pound lock, allowing boats to pass through in both directions.

31

SETTING SAIL

The first reliable ocean-going ships powered by the wind were sailed during the Middle Ages. These ships were rigged with two different types of sail – square sails of the type used by Egyptians, Romans and Vikings, and triangular lateen sails that the Arabs fitted to their dhows.

Replicas of the three ships that sailed with Columbus to America cross the waters off the Florida coast.

OCEAN-GOING SHIPS

One of the first ocean-going ships was the caravel, which the Portuguese developed around the 14th century. The three-masted caravel was designed to sail into the wind. The earliest versions were rigged with lateen sails, with triangular fore-and-aft sails set on long, sloping yardarms mounted on two masts. Before long, caravels were built with three masts, with square sails on the forward two masts and a lateen sail on the third.

The lateen sail allowed a ship to take advantage of a wind that was blowing from the side of the vessel. For example, it allowed the ship to tack through offshore winds until the main square sails were raised.

BETTER STEERING

For centuries ships were steered by means of large paddles or oars mounted at the rear of the ship. The sternpost rudder was another great innovation of medieval times.

Columbus's ships

Two of the ships that accompanied Christopher Columbus on his 1492 voyage of discovery across the Atlantic were caravels. The *Niña* and *Pinta* were quicker and much more manoeuvrable than the *Santa Maria*, Columbus's heavier flagship, and were used to explore shallow bays and river mouths. The *Santa Maria*, in fact, ran aground and had to be abandoned.

The stern, or rear, of the ship was lowered and the rudder mounted on the centre line of the ship, rather than at the side. This rudder allowed the ship to be more easily manoeuvred and to make much better use of its improved sail power. Although the Chinese had invented the sternpost rudder

1,000 years earlier, evidence suggests that the Europeans developed it independently.

THE COMPASS

The other great seafaring invention was the magnetic compass. It was discovered first by the Chinese, but again the Europeans probably invented it independently. The compass provided a means by which sailors could check their direction on the open seas out of sight of land and in any weather.

BARRELS AND CHARTS

A number of lesser, but still vital, innovations spurred ship development and exploration in the Middle Ages. Barrels for carrying drinking water on long voyages were much better made than before and navigational charts became available for the first time. The earliest dated navigational chart was produced in Genoa by Petrus Vesconte in 1311 and is said to mark the beginning of professional mapmaking.

A dhow with a lateen sail moves through waters near the Maldive Islands in the Indian Ocean.

Timekeeping

Most people from the medieval period didn't need clocks or watches. Their days were usually governed by the rising and setting of the sun and their years by the changing seasons.

The earliest way of marking time was the sundial, invented in ancient Egypt, which showed time by the movement of a shadow through the course of the day. The water clock, or *clepsydra*, was a means of marking time at night or when clouds hid the sun.

It worked by measuring a steady flow of water into or out of a container, which was marked with a scale to indicate the passage of time as it filled up or emptied. Both methods were used during medieval times.

The mechanical clock

The origin of mechanical clocks is not known. They may have been developed in monasteries where monks were expected to attend prayers at specific times of the day.

The first mechanical clocks, known as turret clocks, were large, weight-driven machines fitted into towers. These early clocks did not have a dial or hands, and indicated the hours by striking a bell.

The oldest surviving clock in Europe is at Salisbury Cathedral in England. It dates from 1386, but there is evidence that it was not the first of its kind. The Salisbury clock strikes the hours. Other clocks were made around the same time at Rouen, France, and at Wells Cathedral, England. These also had mechanisms that struck on the quarter hour.

The mechanism of the clock in Salisbury Cathedral, England.

When the Old Town Clock in Prague, Czech Republic, strikes the hour models of Jesus and his apostles emerge through a door.

SPRINGS IN CLOCKS

Around 1510 German locksmith Peter Henlein invented a clock powered by a spring. It was a major advance in timekeeping because it opened the way to making clocks and watches that were more compact and portable.

MARKING TIME

Early clocks were big, iron-framed structures that marked the passage of time by a large falling weight. The weight was attached to a cord, which was wrapped around a drum. Its fall was regulated by a mechanism known as a verge (or crown wheel) escapement. An arm clicked back and forward, engaging and disengaging the teeth of a gear wheel and allowing it to turn a little at a time.

These clocks were not accurate and were often wrong by as much as half an hour a day. The first domestic clocks were smaller, wall-mounted versions of these large public clocks. They appeared late in the 14th century. Most were bare mechanisms that did not have a case to protect the moving parts from dust.

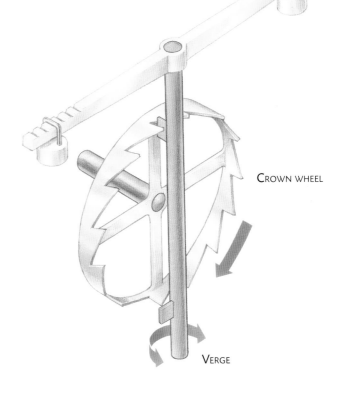

CROWN WHEEL

VERGE

As the vertical verge turns, the crown wheel moves on one tooth at a time.

MEDICINE

Much of the knowledge and practice of medicine in the early medieval period was based on information learned from Greek and Roman texts. The standard of healthcare available varied from people who practised folk medicine to university-trained doctors.

Healing herbs were grown in gardens where they were picked and used for treatments.

THE FOUR HUMOURS

The idea that the body had 'humours' came from the Greeks and Romans. There were said to be four humours: blood, phlegm, yellow bile and black bile. Keeping all the humours in balance was essential for the well-being of a person.

A doctor took a person's pulse and examined their blood, faeces and urine in an attempt to determine what was wrong. For example, blood was checked for different qualities such as hotness, coldness, greasiness, foaminess, thickness and how rapidly it clotted. All this helped the doctor to work out the balance of the four humours in the patient's body.

BARBER SURGEONS

Bloodletting was thought to be a way of restoring the balance of humours and was carried out by unskilled surgeons, who were also likely to be working as butchers or barbers. They also pulled teeth and performed other operations that trained doctors were not prepared to undertake.

The traditional red and white pole seen outside barber's shops in Britain is a reminder

DENTAL CARE

Medieval people cleaned their teeth with herbal rubs and tried to combat bad breath by using herbal mouth washes. A doctor or barber surgeon removed decay from teeth and filled the gaps with ground-up bones – or gold if the patient was wealthy. Loose teeth were strengthened with metal bindings and dentures made from animal bones.

thighs. People with stomach complaints were recommended to chew laurel leaves.

Medieval doctors believed that properties of plants, such as colour, indicated the diseases they were best at treating. Yellow flowers – for example, dandelion and fennel – were linked to the liver's yellow bile and so were used to treat jaundice.

The 'wound man' shows the kinds of wounds that a medieval surgeon was likely to treat.

of the times when barbers did operations. The red represents blood and the white was for bandages used after an operation.

Operations often killed patients through blood loss, shock from the pain or because of infections. Medieval medical practitioners did not know about anaesthetics nor about bacteria and the infections they cause, so no one saw the need to sterilize the instruments used in operations.

HERBAL REMEDIES

Herbal remedies were frequently used to treat illnesses and diseases during the Middle Ages. Common treatments included a mixture of henbane and hemlock that was applied to painful

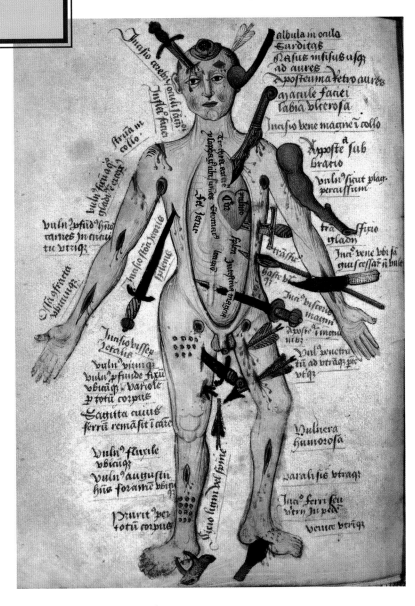

CASTLES AND CANNON

Castles were the homes of medieval rulers and noblemen. They ranged from motte and bailey timber castles to formidable stone structures more like fortresses, protected by a moat and portcullis and defended with cannon.

STRONGHOLDS AND DEFENCES

One of the earliest strongholds was the motte and bailey, which became widespread across Europe in the 11th century. It was a timber tower on a mound (the motte) and encircled by a wall of timber and earth. The grounds enclosed within the wall were the bailey.

Later, castles had masonry walls and towers that enclosed the baileys at the foot of the mound. Beyond the outer walls many castles were protected by one or more moats, which may have been filled with water. Drawbridges across the moats were raised and lowered from inside the castle.

The castle at Foix in south-west France has three distinctive towers.

THE WHITE TOWER

After 1066, William of Normandy built the White Tower to show his authority over his new English subjects. The massive stone castle was 36 metres across and 27.5 metres tall, and was completed in 1100. Over the following centuries succeeding rulers added to the castle and it eventually became known as the Tower of London.

Portcullises defended the entrance to the castle. They were usually made of iron-plated oak and were moved up and down in stone grooves. Openings known as murder holes were created in the roof of the entrance passage. These enabled defenders to hurl missiles down on anyone trying to force their way in. Openings in the floor of the battlements allowed defenders to drop stones or boiling oil on their attackers.

GUNPOWDER AND CANNON

By the end of the medieval period castles were becoming a thing of the past because they could not be defended against the new artillery. The introduction of gunpowder and improved techniques for casting metals, especially iron (see page 25), made cannon and other weapons irresistible.

Gunpowder, yet another Chinese invention, came to Europe in the mid-13th century. It consisted of carbon, sulphur, and saltpetre (potassium nitrate). Saltpetre was made by mixing manure with wood ash, earth and other materials such as straw. This mixture was kept moist with urine for about a year and produced crystals of potassium nitrate.

The first effective cannon was probably made by strapping a number of wrought-iron bars together. Later, cannon were cast in bronze, but bronze was expensive to produce. Eventually, cannon were made from cast iron.

Bombards are a kind of cannon that were used to lay siege to castles and towns.

CAVALRY AND INFANTRY

Knights in armour played an important part in medieval military life. These mobile mounted warriors became an élite fighting force in the wars and battles of the Middle Ages, but by the end of the period they were seen no more.

HORSE AND RIDER

During the Middle Ages, horse riders became more secure and had more control over their mounts because of three important developments. These were the introduction of stirrups, spurs and a wraparound saddle.

The improved saddle was strapped around the belly of the horse and supported a greater weight. As a result it reduced the rider's chances of being unseated in combat. A knight knew that when he rode towards his enemy at speed, and with his lance raised, the impact would not send him flying.

THE LONGBOW

In the 14th century the English longbow was accepted as the premier missile weapon of Western Europe. No one knows how far an accomplished archer could shoot an arrow, but more than 200 metres is likely. Making a longbow from yew wood took as long as four years. The wood was first dried for one to two years, then slowly worked into shape.

This suit of cavalry armour was probably made in Augsburg, Germany, around 1500 AD.

The famous victory of an English army of longbowmen over mounted French knights who outnumbered them at the Battle of Crécy on 26 August 1346 brought an end to massed charges of armoured cavalry on the battlefield.

THE CROSSBOW

From about the middle of the 9th century the crossbow became more and more important to the armies of Europe.

The crossbow was a successful weapon because it was light and portable, and its bolt could pierce the armour of mounted horsemen. Equipping and training soldiers to use crossbows was easier and cheaper than providing cavalry with armour and horses.

Longbow archers fired arrows further and more accurately than any crossbow, but only after years of practice. The crossbow was relatively easy to master and so was very popular until the coming of firearms, such as the musket, in the 16th century.

HALBERD AND PIKE

A halberd had a two-metre long shaft and an axe blade topped with a spike. At the Battle of Morgarten in 1315, Swiss soldiers learned that a man with a halberd could defeat an armoured knight on horseback. The Swiss replaced some halberds with the pike, which was twice as long and had a metal spearhead. A hedgehog formation of bristling pikestaffs easily defeated a mounted assault or advanced through enemy infantry.

The Swiss Guards, who protect the Pope in the Vatican, wear distinctive medieval armour and uniforms, and carry halberds.

Medieval Timeline

410 The Visigoths conquer Rome.

500 The heavy plough is introduced to Europe.

c.700 The stirrup and the horse collar come into use.

711 Muslims called Almohads invade Europe from north Africa.

725 In England, a monk known as the Venerable Bede introduces the system of dating according to the Christian era, ie AD (Anno Domini – in the year of our Lord).

732 The Muslim expansion into Europe is halted at the Battle of Poitiers, France.

793 The Vikings from Norway and Sweden start their raids on Britain and other parts of Europe.

800 Charlemagne is crowned emperor in Rome. This marks the beginning of a rule that will become known as the Holy Roman Empire.

871 King Alfred halts the advance of the Danes in England.

959 England is unified under King Edgar.

c.1000 The whippletree comes into common agricultural use.

1016 King Cnut (Canute) is ruler of England, Norway and Denmark.

1066 The Normans conquer England.

1095–1099 Christians from western Europe fight the first Crusade to recover their holy places in the Middle East.

c.1100 The first universities are founded in Europe at Salerno, Bologna and Paris.

c.1100 The first tidal mills are built.

1140 Knowledge of magnets and magnetism reaches Europe.

c.1150 Compasses are being used in Europe.

1154 Work begins on Chartres Cathedral, France.

1185 The first record of a windmill being used in Europe.

1187 The Muslim ruler Saladin captures Jerusalem from the Crusaders.

c.1200 The horizontal loom is introduced.

1236 The Mongols invade Russia. Five years later they invade Poland, Hungary and Bohemia.

1275 Venetian traveller Marco Polo arrives in China.

1285 Spectacles are invented in Italy.

c.1300 The first cannon are used in Europe.

1348 The Black Death sweeps across Europe.

c.1350 The first blast furnaces are built in Sweden.

1445 Johannes Gutenberg prints the first book in Europe.

1453 The Byzantine Empire falls when the Ottoman Turks capture Constantinople (present-day Istanbul).

1492 Christopher Columbus 'discovers' the New World.

c.1500 The Italian Renaissance begins.

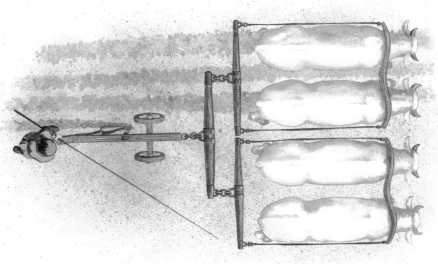

GLOSSARY

adze A carpenter's tool with an axe-like blade mounted at right angles to the handle.

alloy A mixture of two or more different metals. Bronze is an alloy of copper and tin.

anvil A large block of stone or metal used as a support for hammering objects.

apprentice Someone who works alongside an expert in order to learn a trade.

blast furnace A furnace for melting iron ore.

buttress A support, usually on the outside wall of a building.

cast iron Iron made by pouring molten iron into a mould.

crank A handle for turning a shaft.

cruck One of a pair of curved timbers used to support the roof of a building.

daub A mixture of mud and straw that filled the gaps in a wattle and daub house.

draught animal An animal used for pulling heavy loads.

driveshaft A shaft that transmits motion from one part of a machine to another.

earthenware A common type of pottery.

escapement A device in a clock that controls the rotation of its gear wheels.

furrow A long, shallow trench in the ground made by the blade of a plough.

gears A series of toothed wheels arranged so that one turns another.

impurity Unwanted substance in a mixture.

lampblack A type of soot, also called carbon black, used to make ink and pigments.

lathe A tool that spins wood at high speed while it is cut using chisels.

lime A substance produced by burning limestone in a kiln and used to make mortar.

limestone A type of rock.

microorganism A living thing that is too small to be seen without a microscope.

millpond A pond that provides water to turn a mill wheel.

mortar A mixture of cement, sand and water used by builders to bind together stones and similar materials.

navigation The process of planning and following a route from one place to another.

plinth A line of stones at the base of a wall.

ploughshare The main blade of a plough.

quarry An open pit from which minerals and ores are mined.

quicklime Another name for lime, so-called because it was quick to stick to the skin and cause burns.

Renaissance The period of European history at the end of the Middle Ages when there was a great revival in culture and learning.

seasoned timber Wood that has been left to lose moisture before it is worked.

tack Changing direction in a sailing boat to keep the sails filled with wind.

treadmill A mill powered by men or animals that turn a wheel by walking inside it.

trip hammer A hammer that is raised and then allowed to fall by the power of gravity.

type A small metal printing block with a raised letter or character on one end.

wattle A mat of woven sticks used to make the walls of a wattle and daub house.

weir A dam used to create a millpond.

winch A device for lifting or hauling.

withy A strong flexible stick.

wrought iron Iron worked by hammering.

yardarm The horizontal beam on a mast from which a sail is hung.

FURTHER READING

The Early Middle Ages: Europe 400–1000 by Rosamond McKitterick (Oxford University Press, 2001)

Medicine in the Middle Ages by Ian Dawson (Hodder Wayland, 2005)

The Middle Ages 1154–1485 (British History) (Kingfisher Books, 2007)

Medieval World by Philip Steele (Kingfisher Books, 2006)

Daily Life (Medieval Realms) by Peter Chrisp (Hodder Wayland, 2005)

Medieval Castle by Margaret Mulvihill (Franklin Watts, 2006)

WEBSITES

www.mnsu.edu/emuseum/history/middleages/
Medieval Europe: a guide to different aspects of the lives of people in Europe during the Middle Ages.

www.bbc.co.uk/history/british/middle_ages/
An introduction to some of the important people and events in medieval Britain.

www.kathimitchell.com/middleages.htm
The Middle Ages for Kids: a comprehensive list of links to medieval topics.

http://www.engr.sjsu.edu/pabacker/history/middle.htm
Technology in the Middle Ages: including the development of technology in the medieval period.

www.library.csi.cuny.edu/dept/modlang/talarico/medlist.htm
The Medieval and Renaissance Internet: electronic resources for medieval and Renaissance studies.

INDEX